Thistle and Brilliant

poems by

Wren Tuatha

Finishing Line Press
Georgetown, Kentucky

Thistle and Brilliant

ACKNOWLEDGMENTS

The following poems were first published by these journals, sometimes in
slightly different forms:

Thistle and Brilliant, *Midnight Circus*
Folding Chair and Cornbread, *The Cafe Review*
Wicker Me, *Lavender Review*
Big Talking Rocks, *Lock Raven Review*
Leaping Cotton, *The Blotter Magazine*
April in Myth, *Antiphon Poetry Magazine*
Addah Belle's Pocket Watch, *The Bangalore Review*
Maybe a Metronome, *Pirene's Fountain*
Beer Moth Sketch, *Clover, a Literary Rag*
4 a.m., Geneva and Raccoon Abroad, *Flumes Literary Journal*
Cardamom Apparitions and Shiny Things while Waiting, *Peacock Journal*
The Thud of Escapement, *Burningword Literary Journal*
Specific as a Seed, Avatar Review
Not a Promise, *The Bedford Gazette*
Orangesplaining (as Peter with Oranges) and Thuya, *Arsenic Lobster*
Your Violin, *Picaroon Poetry*

Publisher: Leah Maines
Editor: Christen Kincaid
Cover Art: Jenn Zed
Author Photo: Wren Tuatha
Cover Design: Elizabeth Maines McCleavy

Printed in the USA on acid-free paper.
Order online: www.finishinglinepress.com
also available on amazon.com

Author inquiries and mail orders:
Finishing Line Press
P. O. Box 1626
Georgetown, Kentucky 40324
U. S. A.

Table of Contents

to my
constantly talking/cinnamon toast/consensus trainer/
cuddly toy/cosmic trucker,
Cotton,
C.T. Lawrence Butler

Introduction

Thistle and Brilliant is about relationships in motion, as no romantic partnership is static. I never considered depicting the more salacious stereotypes of being bisexual and polyamorous, some drama in which my multiple lovers of various genders play out pleasure and conflict. Instead I'm drawn to snapshots over decades with different partners as each story arcs. Some of my writings from *Hippie Chick Diaries* help set the tone:

Pilgrim of this Moment (Beginnings)

Gurrlfriend/boifriend, speaker of bottle rocket fears, what else can that mouth do? I am edgy tickled you have landed here for a while. Welcome to the possibility that you might get what you need even as you protest that you may not want it/trust it/taste it.

Here's my forest hut. It smells like pond dogs and sounds like a birdcall relaxation CD. Take or leave my chore list and warm the hammock with slow streamside breaths. When my work is done I'll squeeze in, listening to you tingle/purr/set off fire crackers of doubt and flow chart scenarios.

It's about this moment. The next will have its way with us. Specific as a seed, a thistle won't grow from the acorn you bring. It's more the site you pick, the depth of planting, getting dirty, a drink of water, respiration, and the waiting.

Breathe presence, like a wordless animal noticing the planet as it turns, then taking another bite of bergamot. Like a pilgrim arriving, the stony muscles of travel loosening with an inhale at the sight of the temple–more honest, quiet and timeless than the brochure could show. Touch me here. Pray this moment. The next will have its way with us.

Candy Wrappers (Endings)

Candy wrappers and unopened bank statements. Handwritten directions to properties for sale, other women's numbers, receipts mapping out the months we traveled, fixed the car, rewired the house, ate out, bought books. He cleaned his car one day when he was about to take a trip. Clutter from his floorboards went into a plastic Giant bag, which I excavate today, under my kitchen table. I'm reclaiming my space/busying my brain now that he's gone for good.

I handle the bag. Papers into a box to send him. Wrappers in the trash. An old pipe and clamp from a car repair off to the barn. At the bottom of the Giant bag, just grit and brown leaves. It's done.

I wash the kitchen floor, hands and knees. I sort shelves of junk, easily letting go of what hadn't been visible to me in years—picture frames I'd meant to use, some CD rack...boxes for giveaway, the classroom, recycling, laundry. The walls themselves step back, admiring the purge, like a decorator hanging large mirrors to give the illusion of expansiveness.

Another waste bucket full. As I pull the plastic liner awkwardly, I see them spread across the trash–Hershey's–those immortal candy wrappers. He's going with me all the way to the trash, getting the last word, sweet talking me as I discard him again.

When Activists Date Each Other (The Fun in the Middle)
He's not sure I should extend my carbon footprint by coming over tonight. He cites writers who point out that monogamy, even marriage, is more sustainable. Divorced couples haul kids between households. Come to think of it, this polyamory thing could become a significant contributor to greenhouse gases!

Perhaps, but so could the piteous groans I emit when I don't get laid. So here's the plan: I'm coming over and I'll drive the speed limit. I'll pick up any hitchhikers on the way and we'll stop every fifteen miles to plant native trees and spay stray dogs. In my current state, I'm not sure how strays contribute to global warming, but I'll spay them for our collective karma. You have your pet issues and I have mine...

When I get to your house, I'll graze locally on your lawn and shrubbery for dinner. Then I'll let you slowly peel off the seven layers of Goodwill clothes I'm wearing because you minimally heat your house. Then, after all these mitigations, we'll commit some serious global warming...

—Wren Tuatha

Thistle and Brilliant

Sweet Thistle, purple
and green. It looks
almost furry
in the brilliant
rising light.
It makes you want
to take it in hand,
despite all you know.

Muppets are such liars.

Folding Chair

I told you then I would take it out back
and kill it with a knife. But I couldn't do it.
You stumbled upon my love today as then.

It's a folding chair, forgotten in the woods,
rusting beside living oaks and rotting, jutting stumps,
unsuitable seats. Your mind tries to pick up its stories
from the air around. A picnicker, a hunter, absent minded
yogi. But stories are noise, excuses. Mute air transmits
this year's bird noise, same as the moment before
and the moment after this chair was left here.

You realize the years, four legs grounded through
snow mounding and hurricanes, the inflating
and shriveling of mushrooms. Fox and mouse,
mouse and beetle, squirrel and squirrel.
Food and urges and panic. I remember loving you.
There was noise.

Mute, awake air, used to being taken in and released,
doesn't suffer seasons or fools, doesn't root for predator
or prey, doesn't pray that you find your own heart
among curly, restless ferns. I still do.

Wicker Me

Wicker me.
Bend me.
Weave me into a rocker and I'll
wait on your porch with your
faithful dog Bart.

Some August night is our blanket.
Park your clogs
and I'll rock you,
creak next to your skin,
cushion you into your ease.

Wavy pool of cricket songs
and horns out on the interstate.
Wicker me into a painting of this.

Big Talking Rocks

I'm moving the muscles to breathe in cold water.
They feel like bone in the effort.

We had the same brand of toothpaste
on the night we didn't speak of the dimming between us.

Snow that doesn't stay.

You kissed me poetically, pulled a story out of me
like a magician's scarf, red then yellow through my throat.

I undressed to expose skin printed with stories
I should have withheld, psychic tattoos with ink

so shiny you were afraid to touch and be branded.
I'm moving muscles to speak of big talking rocks,

monoliths like grandmother trees, who have stories
in whispered radio waves because they stayed.

They speak in hugging colors and purring hum smiles
because they watched while mammoths, raccoons,

wrens and Americans skittered in circles, never avoiding
their fate. Their muscles made them do it while big talking rocks

wrote the mythology of staying long enough for restlessness
to have its season. I brought the toothpaste you use,

season of snow that sticks.

Cornbread

Cotton takes care of me.
I mend and wonder where
a word went as Cotton hops
out of bed, feeds the herd,
showers. I'm late with his
coffee. I have one job as he
capers around, clipboards
and clients' keys, leash
and a dog to walk.

My hours pass in turns of
whiplash and molasses.
I'm glad he's at work,
not watching. We both recall
when I was brilliant.
He soldiers and I try.
Who takes care of Cotton?

He's aged out of his market.
Once six figures, now Cotton
cleans houses. Five today,
done at six. Home at seven
with stories and rags to wash.
Spreadsheets and payroll.
Menu ideas and shopping lists.
Leash and a dog to walk.
Cotton cares into the void.
Tonight he'll make cornbread.

Leaping Cotton

He is cotton on the stalk, all slicing
armor outside, talking politics,
rubbing you wrong. Inside,
he's nothing but a downy bed.
He made it to lay you there
while discussing dogs
and enchiladas, deciding
to hide away for the day.

Our cotton rabbit in the warren
who warns the others of dogs,
owls and black snakes. Why
listen to the old guy…

He's a mouser cat that will always watch
you and never follow you home
because you never
ask.

Shopping lists and spreadsheets.
A call from Kenya. Send cash.
Cotton boils quinoa while cursing
his web host and mumbling that humanity
has been a disappointment.

He's leaping purple in loose cotton
at the dance, interpreting ice
skating moves, beading
every eye in the room
into one necklace, ribboning.

He might as well,
not that anyone would ever
give him credit.

April in Myth

April is old like water, prehistoric, recycled. Womb
and bladder. To my Third World parched skin,
she's America, running the tap. And now in a foreign
hot tub she mothers me, as if she has it to spare.
Water and muscles, air and my salty grief.

April has bloomed before, on schedule, sometimes
an early surprise. She has chased and she's been cupped
to the lips, been drunk in, and done someone's share
of drinking. Me, too, always in August.

On April's flesh tears and kisses evaporate,
leaving shine. On mine, brine, crusty, leaving in cakes
like the ice shelf. I watch it go, with foreboding
that natural disasters will result.

But water and her children won't be possessed.
In time, she does the possessing, pooling foolish souls
like shrimp, pulling us through hurricanes and extinction
and silence from space.

Mammoths, raccoons, wrens and Americans.

Like water, April is old, knows how to crest and trough,
be a beating organ of the beast, a good germ on the living
planet. Some herons are like pterodactyls pulled by hunger
too far from shore. There are fools and there are fish.
Drink, says April. Extinction breeds myth.
And oh, what a magnetic myth we make.

Addah Belle's Pocket Watch

Addah Belle's pocket watch stands open
on my desk like a sandwich board
advertisement.

I want to shrink down and crawl under it,
camping in my ticking tent. Constellations
and bug spray.

Addah Belle knew me. She could
look at me and tell my future. In her time,
women married.

Addah Belle chose door number two
and taught at a girls' finishing school,
finishing them off for the altar.

Retirement came abruptly. Bourbon and
ceremonies. The stillness of her room
in the farmhouse. And no Marian.

Two twin beds, like a dormitory, and her
married sister downstairs with grandkids on
long weekends.

I, her grand niece, tracked in
with pocket frogs, too-close best
friends and notebooks. She noticed.

Mom cut my unattended hair short.
Strangers took me for a boy. A boy
with notebooks. Listening to Auntie.

And the pocket watch tent would ticka tick,
flashlights and ghost stories on her desk while
she advised I could be a writer, plan a career.

In her time pocket watches were for men.
That might be how it came to her. Tom,
the last at bat who walked home

lost, wondering why she wouldn't
marry him, why remaining at school with
Marian was preferable. The watch

forgotten on a wash stand, a library shelf,
a parlor bridge table. *Tempus abire tibi est.*
     [It's time for you to go away]
The watch she kept and wound, for the sound.

I was a writer when she died. I was a lesbian
when I found her love letters. Her watch,
a flashlight and a tape measure in my drawer.
Tempus vitam regit.
     [Time rules life]

Maybe a Metronome

The work is done, anyway.
You dragged me out of my cave, just by your scent,
and the you I attached to it.

And so I lost weight, remembered I had hair,
styled it. I bought clothes in case you noticed.
You might have. I studied your movements,

as if you were a constellation I would join
in the velvet blanket, as if you were a timepiece,
maybe a metronome, hearing me sing and chord.

You might have, but you couldn't admit it.
You had momentum and flow.
You had a passport and I had a cave.

So I am alone still, but the work is done.
Some other lonely hunter will swirl around
the kill you missed in your momentum,

the corazon you crushed in your flow.

Beer Moth Sketch

Some chatty garden moth, playing in paints,
performing for others, going too far.
He's sorry now, frantic for a plan
that forgives even his dripping sins.

But what a masterpiece he's made of himself.

He is broken light, a bent butterfly,
and he dances doodles in front of me, beauty off kilter,
unready to land, unable to feed.
I can't fix it. Am I supposed to look away?
I can't fix it now.

Am I supposed to move into my next
moment, as if I hadn't seen light, broken,
prisming through sulphur air until his leaded colors
pool on the pavement? Others step around

without slowing, as if his mess were
spilled beer on the street, their favorite beer,
regrettable, but available at the corner store.

Drips of brilliance, beaded childhood colors,
a painter's sweat. The one who painted him
broke him. Tempera thick colors on gossamer pieces.
I can't fix it now. Tripping off kilter, I wish he looked
like beer to me.

4 a.m., Geneva

It's a brute and it's abrupt,
concrete step, cold in summer,
4 a.m., Geneva. Sterile gowns
being unloaded beside me.
Guess they've learned to leave
the grieving alone on this shift.

It's the most complete thought I've
had in an hour. If I don't take the next
breath, the next moment won't have
to come, the one without you in it.

I might go back upstairs, slide my
palm under your fingers like a plate, wait
for the quiver that comes, might come
if I don't breathe.

Why isn't everyone screaming their
heads off? Why don't the floors
buckle and the walls bleed? I should
have stayed longer, held you longer.

Simone, Simone. If I mantra your name
you'll freeze with me. We'll think of
something. I'll will this through.
Doctors will do. Something.

I've made it as far as the loading dock.
Simone, if you're not going to breathe,
I'll have to. The baby only knows
breathing and screaming.

Raccoon Abroad

The raccoon abroad
washes her catch in bourbon
before she eats.

She struts to bass beats
and looks about. Shiny things
are everywhere.

She gypsies and swings,
and his eyes are the skyest
blue, faceted, yet with

no refraction of feeling.
A chainsaw clutch can be
the sweetest ringing bell,

held by the fingertip gently,

and the raccoon abroad
can play the woman
of mystery, revealing

choice shiny things of her own.

Saniya, Scent and Memory

You are the moment I reached the gape
of the Grand Canyon. You're that waterfall
in Cumberland Gap where even the birds
stop to listen to the frozen, flowing moment.
We're slaphappy, like a flock of my friends
tickling and chasing on summer break, 1975.

When you tell me about your day your eyes
gape and grin. I realize I'm doing that mirror
game from acting class. I serve our stir-fry,
picturing that 10 years forward I'll smell
this steam and flash of you. Will I turn
and tell you about it?

Sketches of the Falling Away

Words are thin.
Don't paper me at midnight when the truth
is you're leaving. Don't start a fight to make
the leaving right. Keep me
in your eyes instead, cunning, murky,

devoted. Where your eyes land I am the shard
of want, the fabric in your grasping
hand. You wear me and no change of season has you peeling
me back. You travel, to find
what I am not,

you take me.
These are the things falling away.
Quickness in our pulses, sympathy of our
eyes for each other, dances without obvious music.

This is my skin, continuous with only itself.
My room, a box of stillness and furniture
that knew you.

Breath comes like the turning
of a motor with the oil all burned off.

There's no way the next one could be better.

Cardamom Apparitions

Now Blindness asks, What's in a photograph?
That bending scent—your garden, ripe with dew.
Your softball scar! My gawky dyke giraffe!
Some laughter echoes, tracing down our youth.

The card'mom ghosts that clung to kitchen air.
House renovations—rainbow gingerbread.
The peachy rinse that clouded your roped hair.
Accordion folds...your grin, the sheets, our bed.

Apartments old and brittle, photographs.
So clingy to the touch...Prints left behind.
Your book unshelved, you cradle it—new calf.
Between the slips you visit wilder times

without me. I turn off light's waterfall—
Your skin my album...my state...sweet recall.

The Thud of Escapement

It comes to me in the watch museum.
It's weights, hammers and gears.
Action, reaction.
The thud of an escapement.
The dominoes of a story.

I stand inside a pocket watch
and lose myself to inevitable design.

A plan well engineered
leaves nothing to emotion but the joy
of cog after cog, falling in track,
ticking toward the unalarmed achievement

of another hour struck. Zen empty time.

Our story is like a watch,
weights, hammers, gears.
Little gears for instant gratification,
Huge gears that circle in years with minute changes.

And I know that your actions are reactions,
along a path which matters like another hour struck.
Nothing personal.

Specific as a Seed

Specific as a seed,
not an oak if it's a holly,
my next poem will break
your heart. You will see
a sunrise for the first time
and be still with your coffee
and your breath, remember
the gloves you left
at Brenda's. You'll revisit
a poem on film
and your polemic
over my pet chicken.
You will see a sunrise
for the first time
as a canyon fire,
out of control,
and you will buy
a ticket home.

You, standing in my
yard, will be to me
as specific as a seed.

Shimmer

Shimmer Sharon Shimmer.
Such sunsmile on the water.
I, the shore,
I go to cup her in my hands
and Shimmer she,
she ripples away.

Not a Promise

I
This is not a promise,
just a flaky muse—
What if I give you peaches, cut to the pit
just at the moment of sugaring,
and you shiver when the juice tracks your chin,
amused to be sticky again?

II

I show up with goldenrod
and you've been pondering that empty
corner in your kitchen.

Perfect, or are you allergic to wilderness
and gifts that show up, riding a beaming smile
as if you'd asked the universe a question?

III

Funny how the badminton shuttle rights itself
with each hit. The sight of you chattering,
restringing my racket, content across the net.

My serve...

What if the night sounds of my house become
familiar and you sleep eight hours, your hand
food on the plate of mine, feeding us rest?

You could plant tomatoes while I weed.
Wineberries, catnip, tearthumb.
A notion. Could be shiny.

I laugh that we can't get more than five volleys
of that shuttle off before I miss. I practice but the weight
of your gaze on my hair distracts.
What if I got the rhythm?

Your serve…

Ode to a Cheap Shoe

You're a cheap shoe,
a K-Mart ingenue,
white sole, synthetic smile,
sloppy laces fated to fray,
sloppy canvas that bleeds my socks.
Always complications!

I've been lucky enough
to find just my size
and then the surprise
of an enjoyable fit.
A one season shoe,
no presumptuous spring
in your step,
bouncing back
from the perils
of pavement.
You give in at the toe, heave ho.
And I out grow, and,
Dear John, move on…

Orangesplaining

I'll pivot. Thanks for the oranges and advice.
The citrus of it drips on the latest patch

of my same old rash. Tart, picked early for import,
maybe. But they boost me.

You, picky Peter in the pond, treading water and explaining
the one cylinder diesel engine while I-as-Lorelei swim

naked circles around you, pond moss in my dreadlocks,
in your beard. Hikers on the arteries divert their eyes.

We are organs of that larger hungry animal.
You can be the brain, if it would please you.

I'll be belly lungs, goddess of the yoga
breath. And words, for me, will cease to be symbols,

just handsome howls and organic grumps.
A citrus corsage over a splinter.

Women Are Mountains Scattered

Red pill/green pocket/squire, asks then takes anyway;
can you see me or the planet from a crag in Arkansas?
Gynic peaks pull the moon in you by a string.

What do you orbit? How do you know when to alight if land
and women are mountains scattered, grounded but shifting
unfinished? You and Mohammed, playing pipes at mountains.

Two peaks, one in Africa, the other Appalachia, pour
water that makes the moonbow, marrying light and vapor.
Only two places on Earth does the moon lay this lyric.

Mountains in Nepal listen to gunfire. In Kentucky they
lay down for clean coal, rebranded. Lung forests in Sierras
truck downhill. Peaks in Switzerland take the breath away,

rare oxygen. Do you see me on the planet from Alps, Everest
or Kilimanjaro? Rice terraces and the perfect elevation
for quinoa. Who are you feeding? Who comes to the table?

Not women. When restless we erupt, rebranding, renewing.
We sway slow on our plates. My skin has regrown after lavas.
Sit down. Your babbling is corrosive, a tune in smoke while women

chisel, turn spokes. Narcissus drowning and other irrelevant kings.
No matter your heights, a king convinced of his wings and his view
brought us to this ledge.

Thuya

Thuya, my co, you're a seed airborne,
then a fallen giant, demanding to be mourned,
consumed right here.

You wander, forgotten god, bitter, then liberated
in strong human form, roots gone to feet, then squat
to plant yourself in your mystified, gnarled opinion.

You contort, give me whiplash—I'm dancing, I'm thrown
to ground. We live motion, then the motion was a lie and
we burrow for the frost line. Debate goes to action and a shovel.

Somewhere, lifetimes ago, a tree got his wish.
Now in regret and better wisdom you wander, look for that hole,
a wounded surface that matches the line of your leg.

Until then all your wandering and dancing are for a grave,
dogging you on, threatening rot.

Your Violin

When you look at me your ancestors fall out your eyes—
Romania, the Camps, Zion and Lady Liberty.
You are traveling still, I may not be home.

You look at me when you've found a crack
in your grandmother's violin. Your fingering
stops in the stream as your son bows still.

Your china shop bull prances in my living room.
My grandmother's candy dish clanks/claps in time
or on the edge of it. You would build a village

with words/playing cards/particles, electrons,
if you could just learn the trick of pulling them through
the veil. The veil to that dimension, the veil between

the worlds of the living and dead. Ancestors, reduced
to Platonic forms in your head, to thoughts of a violin bow

as she sings old notes, and remembers leaving home.

When you pull at me your ancestors fall out your eyes
and you become all ages of a human man, out of order
as your face squints affection and worry. *Impish*,

the word you prefer for the boy who makes you say
the wrong thing. And a moment later you're a lover
at my neck or the traveler at mid-life, a highway the neck

of a violin. Thoughts veil your face and your fingers twist
your beard. I expect a Torah lesson but then you return to me
and the boy grins, hands full of liberty and my locks.

You hide in science as if God has hidden your homeland
in space time and we are to live in the house that experimentation
built. I just want to collect your DNA. For further study.

I'm a witch. I know the power of words better than a physicist.
But I'm a poet. I know words are sirens, and a ship on the rocks
is no homeland. But our eyes locked, telling myths we make
to hold hurts, our eyes locked, our bellies locked,

dimensions, homelands, make me your violin.

Gin Bottles

We know this secluded warm pool
and every time my plane lands
we agree by looks to dip deeper.

I mark my mother's gin bottles,
afraid to see the levels go down. Mark
my skin as the water climbs us.

There's a breath-held thrill that fear might
come as a cold current. Not so far,
and you dip me in the words I love you.

Not a splash, just some interplay of water,
waves and sound waves. Time spiraling
unnoticed as we give space and touch.

How do I mark this? Fear asks.
I know you mean it as another holon holding
me against my own demon towel. I'll take it.

Gin bottles. I drink fear like cough syrup.
Believe I can breathe underwater
and our warm pool is space, silently expanding
after the big bang that doesn't hurt a bit.

Sleep Harbored
(after The Accidental Tourist)

You think there's a traffic rule, if you see a sign
for an airport you have to pull in and get on a plane.
It isn't on my way and I don't have the fare.

I sit in my driveway and read your articles from Lima,
Belfast, Shanghai. Weather and lights. Unexpected place
settings and traffic patterns.

I picture your skill at packing a suitcase, adjusting
to time differences with pills and naps, cafe
conversations.

If you are to birth a new beginning you must be judicious
as to the articles you pack, only versatile, lightweight things.
Belongings you won't miss if lost.

But even lost things chance upon new lives with random
finders. The umbrella, the apple core. A quarter. The picture
of her you pack.

A plane flies over my garden near the airport
as I bury what you discarded in the cover crop and leaf litter,
compost.

If you travel here, will you push away vines and mushrooms
to recognize what grows where you left me standing?
Will you profile it as a point of interest?

Sleep harbored.
Random finders can claim you, too.

Shiny Things while Wintering

Me wintering, wise little raccoon,
impatient, blood-drained fingers licking room

temperature tea and neglected dreadlocks.
Sorting yellow seeds from poppy seeds,

poppy seeds from dirt. I hear her typing characters
per second, pining for summer shiny sweat.

Short den days, bringing haiku and didgeridoos.
Shiny things. Knobs to turn and regret.

Spilling and more things to sort. Light kisses
her calendar and we have colored markers,

pix and a plate of pearly mung beans. Shiny
prism in her eye so close that her open mouth

is sifting me in like plankton. Hazel, her eyes
are glycerin. I surrender my skin to her nutrition.

Additional Acknowledgements

Wren thanks these tireless friends, and scores more unnamed, for their work, support, and inspiration with this collection:

Peg Finnie, Patti Hall, Jean Cushman, Kristin Masbaum at Moonlight Novels, Paul Belz, Karen Stupski, Erika Kretzmer, James Handley, Debi Brady, Addah Belle McClaskey, John Thornberry, Tiva, Maria Mazzenga, Eliot Jacobson, Robert A. Garner, Jenn Zed, Maggie Flanagan-Wilkie, Trish Saunders, Roger Fenton, Lavonne Westbrooks, Tracy Mitchell, Tim J. Brennan, Sergio A. Ortiz, Linda Serrato, Robert Chancey, Muir Hughes and The Bookstore, Ramona and John Buck, Heathcote Community, Ganas Community, Jerry D'Amaro, David Seeley, Debby Sugarman, Beth Garner, Kathryn McCann, Winston Plowes, Sydney Wilde and Dennis Daniel, Scott Mize, Betsy Hodgson, Monique German, Susan Wooldridge, Spangle McQueen, Betsy Mars, Donna Hilbert, Risa Denenberg, Kenneth Pobo, Kathy and D.H. Grumbles.

W ren Tuatha is founding editor of the literary journal, *Califragile*. Her poetry has appeared in *The Cafe Review, Canary, Peacock Journal, Coachella Review, Baltimore Review, Pirene's Fountain, Loch Raven Review, Lavender Review* and elsewhere. She was previously Artist-in-Residence at Heathcote Community. Wren studied education at University of Louisville, and film and poetry at Towson University, where she minored in Gay and Lesbian Studies. She received grants from Towson University's Women's Center and Office of Diversity to perform her slam play, *This Is How She Steps on Snakes*, and other productions. Wren is pursuing her MFA at Goddard College. She won a Young Authors Award for Poetry. Wren and her partner, author/activist C.T. Lawrence Butler, herd skeptical goats in the Camp Fire burn zone of California.

CPSIA information can be obtained
at www.ICGtesting.com
Printed in the USA
BVHW030952260819
556811BV00002B/317/P

9 781635 349610